JUNETEENTH
HIGH SCHOOL

SOCIAL STUDIES WORKBOOK

ISBN: 979-8-9901854-4-9

UNTRADITIONAL PUBLISHING COMPANY, LLC

ST. LOUIS, MO

ORDERS@THEACHIEVERSBOOKS.COM

THEACHIEVERSBOOKS.COM

The Achievers Book Series

Untraditional Publishing Co, Est. 2011

Grades Pre-K to 1

Foundational Skills

GRADES PRE-K TO 1

FOUNDATIONAL SKILLS WORKBOOK

Look Inside

Grades 1 to

Reading Literature

THE ACHIEVERS ELA WORKBOOK

Look Inside

For the workl
get all five bo
or mix and m

Grades 3 to 5

Reading Literature

Look Inside

Look Inside

GRADES 3-5
ROADTRIP BROS ELA WORKBOOK

GRADES 3-5
FESTIVAL FRIENDS ELA WORKBOOK

Grades 6 to

Social Studies

Look Inside

JUNEENTEEN
MIDDLE SCHOOL SOCIAL STUDIES WORKBOOK

JUNETEEN
HIGH SCHOOL SOCIAL STUDIES WOR

JUNETEENTH
ELEMENTARY SCHOOL SOCIAL STUDIES WORKBOOK

- Four disciplines
- C3 Framework
- For social studies requirer
  only the workbook is neec

TABLE OF CONTENTS

Name _____   Date _____

WHAT IS JUNETEENTH

Juneteenth celebrates the freedom of humans, primarily of African descent. The holiday symbolizes the end of generational, chattel slavery when people were held against their will.

Freedom is the ability to act, speak, or think as one wants without restraints.

America is known as The Land of the Free. **What are some things you did this week that would have been illegal if you were enslaved?** (example: read). List below:

_____

_____

_____

_____

_____

_____

Name _____   Date _____

JUNETEENTH & INDEPENDENCE

Juneteenth (June 19, 1865) celebrates the freedom of people who used to be enslaved. The Declaration of Independence (July 4, 1776) marks the separation from Great Britain. Both holidays celebrate our freedoms.

Circle the quotes from the Declaration of Independence that support the celebration of Juneteenth:

ALL MEN ARE CREATED EQUAL

[THE RIGHT TO BE] FREE AND INDEPENDENT STATES

[PEOPLE HAVE A RIGHT] TO LIFE, LIBERTY AND THE PURSUIT OF HAPPINESS

[AGREEING TO JUST] LAWS IS WHOLESOME AND NECESSARY FOR THE PUBLIC GOOD

 **Pretend that you turned 18 years old today. Write your Declaration of Independence and the rights you have as an adult:**

_____

_____

_____

_____

_____

Name _____   Date _____

UNION AND CONFEDERATE STATES DURING THE CIVIL WAR

The Civil War, where the Union fought against the Confederacy, was from 1861 to 1865. The primary focus of the war was the economic and moral issues around slavery. The result was freedom for the millions of humans who were enslaved.

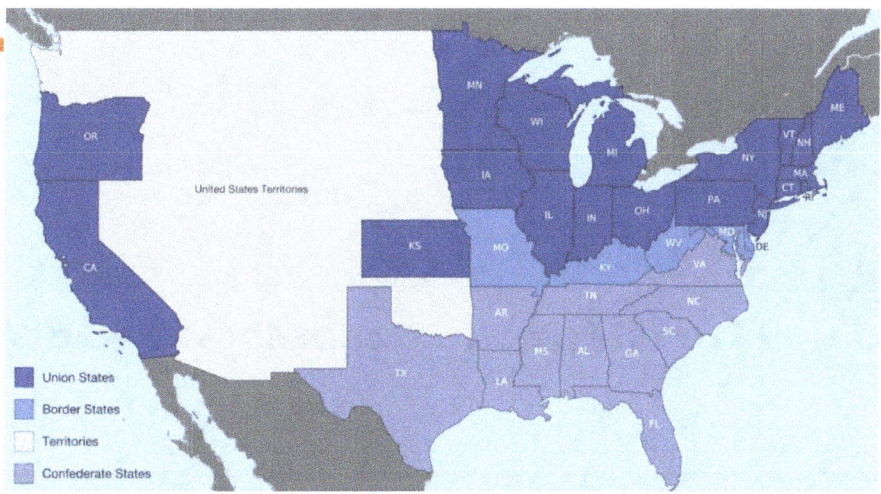

Where were the Union states primarily located?

_____

_____

How did climate play a role in the South's participation in slavery?

_____

_____

Name _____   Date _____

TEXAS STATE MAP

The Emancipation Proclamation
stated that all the enslaved humans were free. It was issued on
January 1, 1863. Then, **the General Order Number 3 was
issued in Galveston, Texas, on June 19, 1865,** freeing the
last 250,000 humans who were still wrongfully enslaved in
Texas. **This day is remembered as
Juneteenth National Independence Day**

Galveston

How would you travel to send a message to Galveston, TX?

_____

Pretend that you were living in 1865. You are newly freed with no house, money, or reading skills. What would you do to survive?

_____

_____

_____

Directions: read the text and answer the question.

Name _____ Date _____

QUOTE FROM GENERAL ORDER NUMBER 3

"The people of Texas are informed that, in accordance with a proclamation from the Executive of the United States, **all slaves are free. This involves an absolute equality of personal rights and rights of property** between former masters and slaves, and the connection heretofore existing between them becomes that between employer and hired laborer"*

In what ways did this order address the moral and economic issues of slavery? In what ways did it not?

Slavery	Moral Issues	Economic Issues
Addressed		
Not Addressed		

*"Juneteenth". Texas State Library and Archives Commission.

Name _____ Date _____

AMENDMENTS & ACTS

In 1865,
the **13th Amendment** abolished slavery

In 1868,
the **14th Amendment** gave citizenship to all people born in the US

In 1870,
the **15th Amendment** gave Black Americans the right to vote

The **Civil Rights Act of 1964** prohibited discrimination based on race, color, religion, sex or national origin

The **Voting Rights Act of 1965** outlawed discriminatory voting practices

How is the time between the **15th Amendment and the Voting Rights Act of 1965** similar to the time between the **Emancipation Proclamation and Juneteenth**?

_____

_____

_____

Directions: read the text and answer the questions.

Name _____   Date _____

TIMELINE

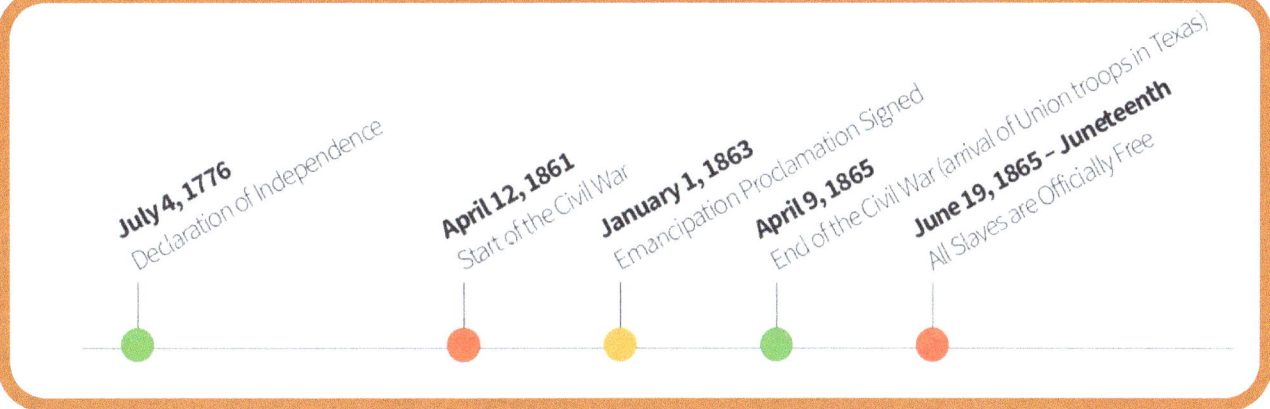

July 4, 1776
Declaration of Independence

April 12, 1861
Start of the Civil War

January 1, 1863
Emancipation Proclamation Signed

April 9, 1865
End of the Civil War (arrival of Union troops in Texas)

June 19, 1865 – Juneteenth
All Slaves are Officially Free

During the time between the Emancipation Proclamation and Juneteenth, there were people enslaved that should have been free. How do you think each group of people felt during this time, and why?

The people who were freed:

The people still enslaved:

Abolitionists (people who wanted to stop slavery):

The people who owned enslaved people:

Name _____ Date _____

OPAL LEE AND BECOMING A NATIONAL HOLIDAY

In 2016, 89-year-old **Opal Lee began her walk from Fort Worth, Texas to Washington, DC** to make Juneteenth a national holiday.

Support grew for making Juneteenth a national holiday. First Lady Melania Trump celebrated it in 2020. Then, President Joe Biden made **Juneteenth a federal holiday on June 17, 2021.**

If given the chance, **what day would you make a federal holiday?** (example: your birthday)

_____

_____

_____

Photo by: David Perry

Name _____   Date _____

JUNETEENTH CELEBRATIONS

The beginning years of Juneteenth celebrations (also called Jubilee Day, Freedom Day, Emancipation Day, etc) included food, singing, and church-centered gatherings. There are so many ways to celebrate Juneteenth today: Party at the park or backyard, festival, live music or dance performance, BBQ, cookout, cook traditional foods, parade, pageant, talent show, outdoor games, make a display of relevant books at a local library, support a local business, reading, movie.

Let's pretend that you are hosting a Juneteenth celebration. Create an invitation:

You're Invited!
Juneteenth Celebration

Day: *June 19*
Time:
Place:
What to Expect:

Name _____ Date _____

HOW WE CAN CELEBRATE JUNETEENTH

Juneteenth brings more opportunities for local black-owned businesses that participate in the holiday. This includes businesses such as event spaces, restaurants, clothing companies, authors, etc. This celebrates the transition from generational slavery to generational freedom and wealth.

1. If you **start a business, what products or services would you offer?**

_____

_____

2. Is there a **local black-owned business in your city?** If so, what are their products or services? (examples: bookstore, I'm not sure)

_____

_____

Name _____   Date _____

TEST YOUR KNOWLEDGE

1. When was the original Juneteenth?	a. June 19, 1865 b. June 19, 1965 c. June 9, 1865 d. June 9, 1965
2. Where was the original Juneteenth?	a. St. Louis, MO b. Jacksonville, FL c. Galveston, Texas d. New York, New York
3. In 2016, this person walked from Fort Worth, Texas to Washington, DC to make Juneteenth a national holiday. What is the name of this person?	a. Oprah Winfrey b. Opal Lee c. Rosa Parks d. Martin Luther King Jr.
4. When did Juneteenth become a federal holiday?	a. June 17, 1865 b. January 1, 1970 c. January 1, 1999 d. June 17, 2021

answer key: 1. (a) 2. (c) 3. (b) 4. (d)

Directions: draw a line to match each amendment to its definition.

Name _____ Date _____

TEST YOUR KNOWLEDGE

13th Amendment

gave Black Americans the right to vote

14th Amendment

gave citizenship to all people born in the US

15th Amendment

abolished slavery

Directions: draw a line to match each holiday to its definition.

Name _____   Date _____

IN YOUR OWN WORDS

What is Juneteenth?

_____

_____

_____

Why was General Order Number 3 issued?

_____

_____

_____

As of today, would you consider America The Land of the Free? Why?

_____

_____

_____